yesterday
i was
the moon

yesterday
i was
the moon

---

noor unnahar

CLARKSON POTTER/PUBLISHERS

NEW YORK

Copyright © 2017, 2018 by Noor Unnahar

Published in the United States by Clarkson Potter/Publishers,
an imprint of the Crown Publishing Group, a division of
Penguin Random House LLC, New York. Originally published
by CreateSpace, Scotts Valley, California, in 2017.
crownpublishing.com
clarksonpotter.com

CLARKSON POTTER is a trademark and POTTER with colophon
is a registered trademark of Penguin Random House LLC.

Library of Congress Cataloging-in-Publication Data is available
upon request.

ISBN 978-0-525-57601-3
Ebook ISBN 978-0-525-57602-0

Printed in the United States of America

Book design by Danielle Deschenes
Illustrations by Noor Unnahar

10 9 8 7 6 5 4 3 2

First Clarkson Potter Edition

for
Amma Jaan and Areeba

DEAR READER,

THIS BOOK IN YOUR HANDS IS
A HISTORY OF FRAGMENTS LEFT
BY A BODY ONLY MOVING FORWARD,
ENTWINED WITH RELIGION AND
PERSONAL GROWTH. IT'S A MEMOIR
IN VERSES, A HOUSE LEFT IN
PIECES AND A HOME GEARING
UP TO BE REBUILT.

LOVE,

NOOR

"How long," they say, "how long, O cruel nation,
   Will you stand, to move the world, on a child's heart,—
Stifle down with a mailed heel its palpitation,
   And tread onward to your throne amid the mart?
Our blood splashes upward, O our tyrants,
      And your purple shows your path;
But the child's sob curseth deeper in the silence
      Than the strong man in his wrath!"

{Elizabeth Barrett Browning, "The Cry of the Children"}

yesterday—i was the moon
today—just an eclipse
something in me travels; some days it's to
the dark
some days it's to
the light

i am building
a house

where the floor is
made up of strength
where the walls are
crafted of ambition
where the roof is
a masterpiece of forgiveness

i am building
myself

my mother's name
translates into
the sun of the women
she named me
noor unnahar
light of the day
i shine when i want to
i burn when i have to
the sun named me light; i know
how to dwell in the sky
with eclipses and stars

{shams un-nisa}

i am the rage
left unspoken
unheard
unfortunately
by the women before me
so i write a lot and speak
a little firmly
giving life to the words that never
made it out of their mouths

i want stars, strength, and balance in my soul
it's been a while since they were last
together in me

to the person who
will want to fall in love with me
i have been a sky all my life
full of life and light and anger
if you're not coming with
thunderstorms; do not come
at all

nothing teaches better
than this trio

the fears, the tears, the years

{the golden trio}

learn to lose
and
it will teach you how
winning works

i envy the sun
that shines at your side
of the world; everything
looks brighter when
two of you rise

in this human skin
i am half war
half peace

people leave
because
unlike matter
that has firm, solid, strong
molecules
people are made up of
air, fire, earth and water
that change shapes
that keep moving
that cannot stop
so let them go
and let them be
the things they want
the shapes they like
because
in the end
you too will grow
into something
entirely new
so let them go

wishlist:

1. tremendous courage
2. the power of forgiveness
3. strength in abundance
4. an unlimited supply of kindness

you are
the peace after wars
the calm after storms
and everything
insanely beautiful
that shapes after
a tragedy

5:30 am
i wake up
dusting away my sins
even the sky is asleep
and calmness greets me; *fajr*

1:50 pm
i finish my chores
find peace on a mat
angry heat is roaming the streets
contentment enters my house; *zuhr*

5:40 pm
i will have my tea soon
but success awaits
in 4 rakats
the sun is now tamed; *asr*

7:00 pm

the light is going
and birds have gone
to their warm little nests
i am praying for home; *maghrib*

8:30 pm

the stars are bright
and they twinkle outside
the window of my room
I am standing in ruku; *isha*

this is how
5 times a day
i am
*authentically, avidly, absolutely
alive*

{namaz}

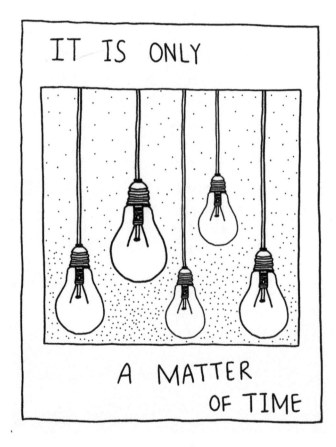

4:12 pm, five years ago, you were younger and you were waiting for a miracle to happen; to change everything. but this world isn't as generous as it appears and there's always a lack of miracles for those who wait for them. but yes, it does extend a hand to everyone who is willing to step forward and stare daringly in the eyes of life to give them their share of miracles.

{you are a miracle}

it only takes
a second or two
to look into their eyes
and decide
whether you're *home*
or at just another
perfectly decorated *house*

when you fall
do it gloriously
collapse like a glass building
sink like a gigantic ship
and when you're done
sinking and collapsing and
sinking and collapsing
build yourself
with your wreckage

NO SOUNDS LEFT

ONLY EMPTINESS

i walk on two bridges everyday
one is easy; like my mother tongue
the other is scary; like a foreign language
it creaks
and my soul is split
between these two bridges
i cannot stop sounding
like the language i grew up with
and i cannot stop speaking
this foreign language
for it helps me
survive

{bilingual}

you'll have to learn
the art of
losing, choosing, and refusing
to win what we call
the game of life

some houses are haunted. but they aren't
always inhabited by ghosts. sometimes some
memories dwell there so starkly, their nameless
faceless sorrow starts taking over and the walls
keeping that house together start to collapse. i
have walked into such houses only to witness a
melancholic past, a withering present and a
silent future. those houses carry the dead
dreams and maybe broken hearts too
because god knows where else one
could ever find this much sadness
that would turn one firm building
into an abandoned mess.

{haunted houses without ghosts}

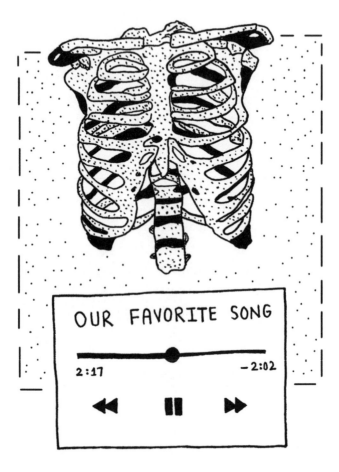

we belong
nowhere and everywhere
to the glimmering streets
of glorious cities
to the dark and dusty alleys
of places with names
that are hard to pronounce
and i wonder
if it is like that
because it's been too long
since i last went home

{nomads}

like the anger of fire
shapes metal
like the sorrow of a writer
creates poetry
everything that is beautiful
doesn't always start
beautifully

i am too afraid
of people who have souls like hometowns
warm, forgiving and too kind
that even if you leave; even when you leave
will always welcome you home
remember you with your family name
i am too afraid
of something too homely
when every breath coming out of my body
is shaped like leaving

{too afraid}

grow
like a wildflower
the one people do not notice
for they don't smell like exquisiteness

and when you know you have
grown into something that is
remarkably exquisite
help those
who are like the wildflowers
that do not smell like
exquisiteness

you remind me of my favorite metropolis
sparkling, loud yet hauntingly sad when
the light goes out
your confidence; a popular skyscraper
your sadness; an old orphanage
your anger; a call of riot
your tears; an uninvited storm
i cannot thank you enough
for reminding me that cities too breathe
and humans too carry a heart of concrete

{my favorite metropolis}

how easy it is
for you to talk about destroying
buildings
plants
people
but i hope you remember
all of them can be rebuilt
from the tiniest pieces of their
remains

YEAH.

isn't it
breathtakingly beautiful
how you've learned
to grow flowers
from the memories
that died
a long time ago

you look like a museum to me

standing firm in a chaotic city
calm in spite of all the urban noise
and beautifully aware of all the art
that resides in you

some of our men have become too large for our houses
that anyone who is not a man looks like
the shape of a foot to them
you're not even equal to my shoe; it sounds
funnier than it actually is
they hope we will shrink—paint ourselves in
delicate frames to hang on the walls
but
we know how to build homes out of their
mortgaged dreams
and if we leave
their buildings will collapse
that is when they will know
we are the size of the skies and
their feet will look smaller than they actually are

{when women become the skies}

my dreams now look like spears
that i have to hold upside down
clench too tightly and i will bleed
hold too lightly and they will fall

there are days when i am a flag of victory
standing firm on a familiar ground; my fabric
without a single crease
winds bringing me pride and attention
from foreign eyes
but such days do not stay and then come
the days of being a flag of surrender
deprived of glory; i stand as a symbol
of what time is capable of doing
that with a new wind
comes a new victor
comes a new victim

{flags}

you are the loudest
and brightest
color of my life
my brushes refuse
to work when
your shade isn't present

{when an artist falls in love}

SOME MEMORIES

sometimes my words
become a pile of broken glass
they do not come out
without hurting; dripping blood
and i forget how to speak

{difficulty}

history
i want it to reflect in my eyes
echo in my words
grown on my skin
for my mirror needs to know
where i come from
where i have been
and where i am going

i share a legacy
with the sky
we both know how to carry
some unanswered prayers
and some unshed tears

{the sky & i}

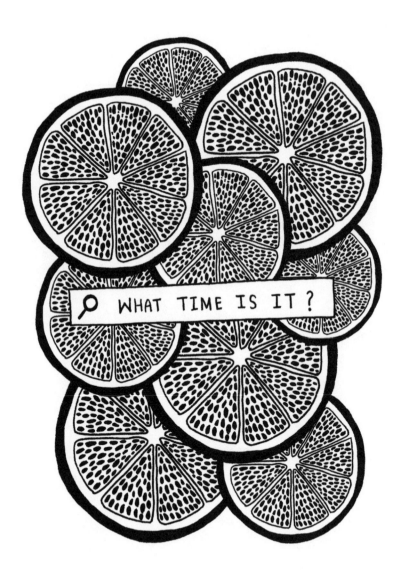

in pieces
yet at peace
i am a building
in a post-war city

{survival}

you're the moon
and the world is
a lonely wolf; it cries
at the sight of you
for you are glorious
and so out of reach

no i didn't forgive you
out of love
mercy or sympathy
i forgave because
i knew i would
need to be forgiven
by someone like me

and if i kept my forgiveness
to myself
in the future
that someone like me
would also keep
their forgiveness
and it would
kill me

{forgiveness}

isn't it absolutely
terrifyingly, shockingly
amazing
how words
those tiny little sounds
in this chemical-filled air
those shapeless weird marks
on stark white paper
can make or break
living breathing people
stab them at heart
without a single weapon
push them off
their strong firm feet
take away the earth
they used to stand on
words; they're powerlessly powerful
so use yours
well

a piece of cloth on my head
screams an identity
louder than words printed
on any document
even the sky outside knows
where i come from

{hijab}

it's okay
if you're burning
with anger
or sadness
or both
it is necessary
for you to collapse
so you can learn
how phoenixes are
reborn
when they burn
and rise again
from the ashes of
their existence

there is a hurricane
inside my ribcage
where a heart
used to be

{change}

my bones carry
calmness and chaos equally
before every war; i sound
like peace
after every fall; i rise
a hurricane-shaped masterpiece

bravery was the lullaby
i was put to sleep with
tangled in my mother's words
it has been an old friend
i hum it in silence; it screams
in me in crowds

i was supposed to be a city
with busy streets and twinkling lights
but i wanted to be a house
full of warm sunlight
and dried flowers gracing its vases
i'm neither today but
a hollow skeleton of progress
where everyday something
builds and collapses
i am happier in this

{a work in progress}

teach your heart
how to not be like glass
it shatters; delicately
a beautiful tragedy
toughen it with fire
of strength and bravery
so it couldn't break
that easily

{teaching survival to my heart}

art doesn't ask
to be perfect
poetic
precise
it asks to exist
to breathe
to be

this is what it has always been about

the most beautiful thing in this world isn't made
up of particles. it's the strength of a person who
has seen the collapse of their world, everything
they held dear crashing down in a million pieces.
yet every morning, they wake up and build their
life, all over again. mourning their loss in a
tranquil silence. i haven't yet seen
anything more astonishingly beautiful.

the price of leaving
is everything
you do not return to a place
but to a memory; soundless
a home becomes another house
a face becomes another name
a city becomes another geographical location
when you leave

my homeland gifted me
a language with soft corners
it feels like sugar in my mouth
and the language i learned to speak
is made up of wax; it often melts
and burns my mouth
leaving my words
soundless
shapeless
helpless
and i cannot help but sound like
someone utterly unknown

{accent}

in my accounting class, we were taught how
to make balance sheets. in those lessons, the
credit part had to be equal to the debit part
for your balance sheet to be complete. it
was beautiful; the balance of everything ever
spent, ever accumulated, ever given. this
concept made me fall in love with balance.
so i learned to balance things in my
life as it would happen in those balance sheets.
if i told a lie, i had to speak a bitter truth
next time. if i spent more than i was supposed
to, i donated some amount to charity
next time. if i said something not-so-nice, i would
find words to say something extra-nice
next time. i learned to pay for things i had
done. i learned to create the balance.

{creating the balance}

last night i whispered
a thank you note to the universe
for it made oceans and stars
equally beautiful and accessible
for all of us; i breathe the same air
as the people i love and the people i lose
the particles of their existence are still
surrounding me and this is how loneliness
doesn't know how to find me alone

{a thank you note to the universe}

home murmurs
where have you been?
and i can't help but say
away; looking for you

when everything comes crashing down
i hope you're wearing
that faint little smile
for an end is near
and a start is nearer

wear your past with grace
present with care
and future with delight
nothing gleams better
when three of them
are carefully combined

you asked me
how i made art
and
i used all
long, shiny, pretentious
words

but the truth
is different
i never made art
i brought the hurricanes
sobs, revenge, stories
on the stark white sheet

and it looked
something like
art

{it was art}

SOMETIMES

SOMETIMES

falling in love with cities is risky.
they'll welcome you with spectacular sunsets
and stunning skyscrapers and a skyline that
lights up the whole sky. but when they're angry,
they will burn themselves down to fuel a riot
that'd run loose on their streets. they will
remind you that if you love a city with
its lights on, you will have to love it
even when it is on fire.

you're not only a *she*
or a *her*
make your name sound
like something
completely terrifyingly, beautifully
out of this world

{azeez aurton—dear women}

some mornings
my hometown breathes in me
my mind: chaotic like its traffic jams
reminding me how i said
whoever leaves first will be free
but when you leave a city
it doesn't mean it will leave you in return
its name forever with mine
mine forever with a city i haven't been to
until it's the time to go
i will return to ask its moon to die
with me; the lights that saw me first
must also see the last of me

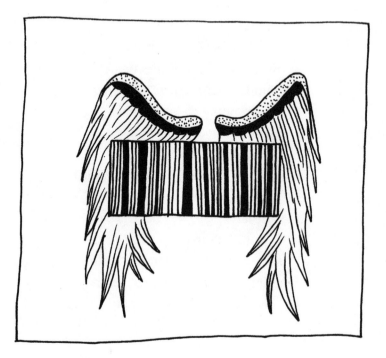

do not worry
about people

they're wearing the same flesh
breathing the same chemicals
walking on the same solid earth
as you

so why should it matter
when
you are them and they are you

the universe is a brilliant writer
it wrote your name
in my stars
before any of us existed
so when the time comes
they'll light up your path
and lead you straight to me

{nikah}

you wanted to know about the art i created and the melancholy behind the words but i couldn't tell you how and why those shades and words found their way on that crisp white graceful paper because sometimes some things do not have a story and artists spill their tears and blood and sweat on a canvas just so we could keep art alive even when we don't have a story telling you *why* because if art were to be explained you would know how empty everything is; from creations to the hearts that created.

{the artists and their art}

THE GROWING ACHE

broken homes produce
walking, talking wars
their residents
either become their own cities
or their own ruins

distance becomes
a name; a living thing; a breathing tragedy
when two people are apart
not by cities or countries or continents
but by the lack of words
and abundance of silence

someday
something
will go
terribly, utterly, horribly
wrong
one day
everything
will be fine

our lives
swing between
that one day
and someday

so why do you worry
about it
everyday

when you've heard the
heartbreak coming
do not close the door

invite it in
make it a big warm mug
of your favorite tea

ask why it came
and ask how would it like
to leave

let your heartbreak know
that it has arrived
at the very wrong door

that the dweller here isn't
afraid of the things
that have been broken before

{heartbreak}

no you don't
have to be all this nice
all this time
scream, break, and shatter
till your lungs have pumped out
all the words you had to swallow
all the pain that froze your blood
all the worries that tainted your skin
and when you're done
freeing yourself
please go and be nice

{before being nice}

sadness

1. it's in the air of the city i loved and left
    to never return. it's the smell of leaving.

2. it's a shapeshifter. it looks like a face i do not
    want to remember. then suddenly it is a face i
    cannot forget. a dishonest performer.

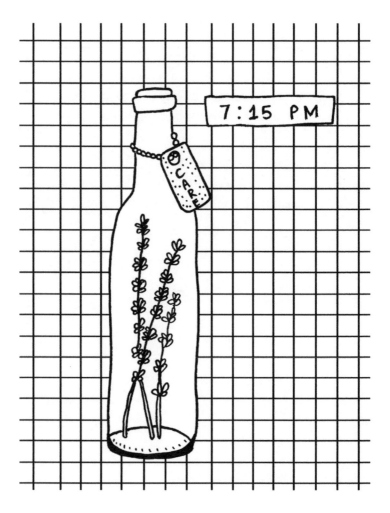

when you've lost everything and everyone,
meet defeat with open arms. shake hands with
it; warmly, firmly, happily. it has taught you all
the things you shouldn't do if you want victory
next time—embrace it. your defeats are not a
sign of your weaknesses; they never were and
they will never be. they are the medals you need
to decorate in your living room for the world to
see so they can know where you are coming
from, because in the end the victor and the
defeated are kind of the same; one has won the
battle and the other one knows how exactly
it is won.

{welcoming defeat}

next time i'm asked
about my confidence that glimmers
and whether it's there in me because
the men of my family were too liberal
i will tell them one thing
the men weren't there when i was growing up
but women
they walk with grace and fire dances
with their cooking pans
their words are loud and eyes even louder;
woven with intelligence and history
the women in my family are shaped with
glass and love wrapped in silk
they teach their kids to speak with
kindness and firmness
so when they speak
they do so without hesitation

{women of my family}

when ache arrives
put it on paper
it is here to hurt your heart
use it to save your art

how dare you call
an arrangement of bricks my home
home is the comfort
built with my mother's words
home is the art piece
my sister hung on the wall
and
home is all the people
who make my heart feel at ease

you had a face
that looked like serenity
and words
that did not smell
of contempt
and your existence
reminded me
of sunsets and ocean waves
yet
you still wonder
what it took
for me to fall
for someone like
you

i fled
forgave and forgot
people

for this hurricane in me
could either ruin
all of them
or save
all of me

and i
chose me

you have been away
from home for so long
in my dreams you look like
a lonely building in a curfew-imposed city

{absence}

strong
is not only a word; it's a compliment
for all the women of my generation
who couldn't be anything
but strong
at a point that
saved their lives

i am fighting
my losses
trauma
and everything bringing ache
because i don't want
to look in the mirror
and see a tragedy staring back

no fire
could collapse the pillars
you have built yourself on
with tremendous artistry
with startling bravery

the sunset looked way too pigmented—as if
the color palette of sorrow had been thrown on
it. yes, if sorrow had colors, they would be lilac
mixed with pinks and some sneaky whites like
the clouds at twilight. i thought it was a
masterpiece; a way for nature to share that at the
end of the day, each sobbed whisper goes
directly to the skies. but before that, it leaves
its color on the canvas of earth one last time.

{the color of whispers}

i am putting together
a future for me
that gleams with the lights
of cities i haven't seen
that exhibits the art
my hands tremble to create
that looks like everything
i haven't written poetry about

{future}

be kind
for this is something
a lot of people
can never be

metal clashing with fire;
this is how anger and i
fight
melt
settle

you said you would stay forever
but does this forever include all the times when
i am an earthquake; tearing apart my
own existence—burying down my own cities
because
i do not want the sound of the word *forever* in
the same air where I keep the sound of the
word *survival* if it was never meant to
be there at all

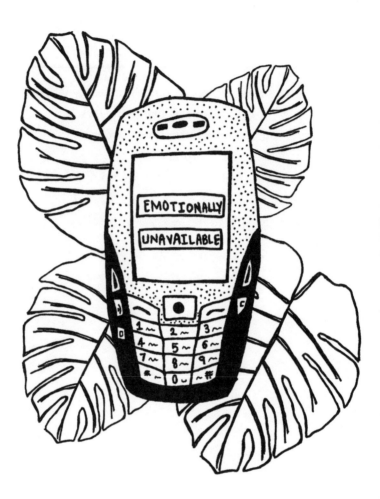

darling
self-discovery isn't always
about the most convenient ways
you'll have to burn, learn, and yearn
the unexpected, the unusual, and the unknown

i carry
the stories
the sadness
the victories
of people before me
i'm both a monument
and a future skyscraper
rising from the same skeleton

{family name}

with this thunder in your heart
and melancholy in your art
there is something
utterly, completely and satisfyingly
perfect about the way you live
this imperfect unpredictable life

i go to a war against words
to fight 'til one of us
has shed enough blood
to accept defeat; there's no
easy way to write

time has woven
courage on my skin
i'll shed myself whole
before it is taken away

{a promise}

the kind people
are running this world
they don't know how
their one little smile
has saved many lives

i want to travel more. and out of a thousand
other reasons, i want to travel to be homesick.
i want to be on another land yearning for the
food of my hometown, for the warm and
aromatic chai my grandmother makes, for the
pink bougainvillea that stands firmly on the
lawn of our house. i want to travel to be away
from home so that i can return, loving it as
much as it deserves to be loved. i want to go
away from home just for returning back here
to realize everything i have ever neglected is
worth loving and
worrying for.

{wanderlust}

confidence is
the greatest armor
i have lost
many battles without it

words
are the antidote
for everything
that's ever hurt
ever stopped
ever bruised
my heart

{a writer's remedy}

BEFORE GOING AWAY
BEFORE GOING AWAY
BEFORE GOING AWAY
BEFORE GOING AWAY

who would have thought
that you
whose bones
have been to battles
whose words
burn before they come out
could be this gracefully composed;
an arrangement of kindness and strength

i am learning
how to say "strong"
in different languages
for if i ever forget
the sound of this word
in my own language
those words
could remind me
there are more
words
chances
worlds
where mine
ends

accept change
it doesn't happen often
for most of us

freedom is really expensive and no one will wrap
it in a fancy paper to leave at your doorstep. you
will have to buy it with the currency of blood,
sweat and struggle. it doesn't twinkle like sparkly
things. it is often shaped like bruised knees
and mourning skin. but what makes it too precious is
the fact that a lot of currencies will never be
strong enough to bid for it. this is where
it becomes insanely priceless.

{freedom}

the idea of destruction
keeps running through my veins like blood
yet my bones hold the will to create
everyday blood and bones in me clash
to create something; to destroy something

{the struggling artist}

a bolt of lightning
striking a building
made up of delicate glass

this is how i visualize
heartbreak

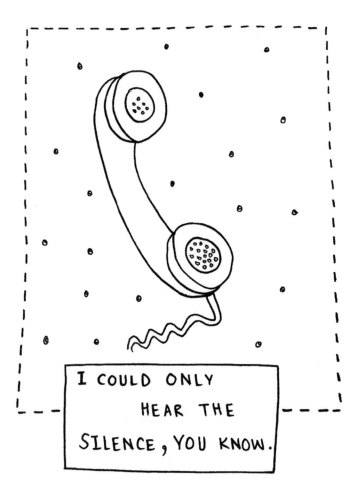

my parents are two long calls
one is about the weather—always about the
weather; father
one is about everything—you should do *this*
this and *that;* mother
cities away i do not calculate distance but
duration
has it been days?
has it been hours? since you last called
you do not get out of a broken family because
it gets out of you; a family in pieces
where their names become a hello and my name
becomes a good-bye
two voices on each side of the phone is what i
have in legacy now

{broken family}

what if we started naming heartbreaks after
people like they do with storms on
news channels
how would this heart look with name tags?
little crack—death; grandmother
a big part missing—departure; nameless
a part that still hurts—origins unknown; you

my heart has become a silent neighborhood
where only emptiness and your name dwell
nobody goes there; nobody gets out
because in a town where the only
thing you can breathe
are memories
nothing lives; nothing dies

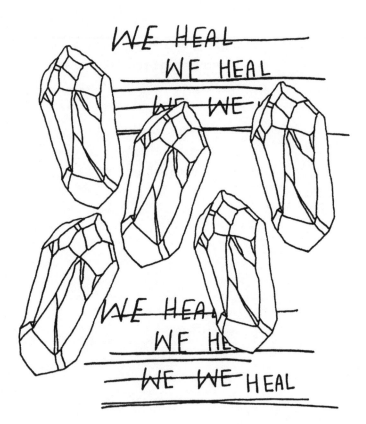

with every sunset
a new hope is born
an old expectation dies

every single dream you've pushed into
the ocean
praying that it dies and leaves you alone
the water carries them; breathing and alive
you left them to wither but their pieces wither in you
dreams live as long as the dreamers do

survival is not beautiful
it is fire, ache, and everything that hurts
combined

but the survivors know how
after survival
everything is so insanely beautiful

i roam around in nameless alleys
taking photos with my kodak
for i am in love with a city
that didn't love me back

i can fix a lot of things
but cannot mend a broken heart
for it is too fragile
and fixing it
is another art

but i hope to learn it soon
as i see mine getting torn
before it breaks into a million pieces
and i am left to fix it
all alone

i am growing flowers
in the darkest part of my heart
for if light ever enters
it would know where to start

my mother named me
light; the first ray starting the day
and there are days
when i forget there is
light at all
this name then becomes
a reminder how
the woman who raised me
named me after something
so glorious; it shines
and even on my darkest days
i am the light i should be looking for

{noor}

thank you for
getting
holding
reading this book
i am grateful

i hope you are taking
strength for your heart and art
from *yesterday i was the moon*
as the end arrives

{author's note}

khatam shud
it ends here